Baseball in the Nineteenth Century: An Overview

JACK SELZER

Published by the Society for American Baseball Research, Inc., P.O. Box 1010, Cooperstown, NY, 13326. FIRST PRINTING — Ag Press, Manhattan, Kansas.

EXPERIMENTATION, INSTABILITY, UPHEAVAL: these words characterize the course of baseball history during the nineteenth century. In a time of rapid urbanization, aggressive individualism, and social darwinism, amateur and professional baseball captured public fancy nationally yet suffered as well the consequences of both cutthroat competition and monopolistic trusts. After codifying a standard game in the 1840s and 1850s, amateur baseball clubs during the 1860s and 1870s fought professionals for dominance in the sport, while the professionals themselves struggled to create a stable entertainment capable of attracting public patronage. Like other businesses struggling through these years of a nation's industrial awakening, the professional game at first consisted of a fragile patchwork of local enterprise searching for an organized structure. By the 1880s, the recently formed National League could count among its blessings exciting competition, new standards of playing excellence, and high profits; but it was also cursed by competition with rival leagues and the claims of dissatisfied players. In the 1890s the National League emerged as the dominant professional league and standards of play continued to improve, but economic reverses encouraged experimentation on the field (in rules changes) and off (in administrative structures). Perhaps Mark Twain was correct in 1889 when he described baseball as "the very symbol, the outward and visible expression of the drive and push and rush and struggle of the raging, tearing, booming nineteenth century." In any case, baseball by 1902 had achieved remarkable stability in its rules, in the hierarchy among its leagues (both professional and amateur), and in its major league franchises — stability that would hold for a half a century.

In the Beginning

Baseball's "creation myth" — that the game sprung fullbodied from the brow of Abner Doubleday one afternoon in 1839 in Cooperstown, New York — is more romantic but unfortunately less reliable than the "evolutionary theory" that has displaced it. In the middle of the nineteenth century Henry Chadwick, who began writing about sports in 1848 and who two decades later was being called "The Father of the Game," tied the roots of baseball to the English game of rounders, which is played by two teams (including pitchers and strikers) on a diamond-shaped field with four bases. Nearly everyone has also noticed the obvious parallels with cricket, a game in vogue in America in the 1840s and 1850s; and others have cited various "old cat" games that, depending on the number of players, involve pitchers and hitters who score by completing a circuit around two, three, or four bases. In short, baseball evolved from multiple sources, and during the first half of the nineteenth century numerous versions of the sport prevailed in a number of communities, large and small, across the young American nation. Such games were informal by nature; the number of participants and the particular rules in force depended upon who showed up to play; and participation, not observation, mattered above everything.

In 1845 a group of New Yorkers who had been playing ball in the Madison Square and Murray Hill sections of the city since 1842 started a fraternal organization, the Knickerbockers, for the purpose of playing baseball and furthering their aristocratic social aspirations. One of the club members, Alexander Cartwright, formally codified a particular variety of the game by composing rules that covered etiquette as much as sport. Intended as a genteel, polite recreation that would serve as a preamble to a banquet or other social occasion, the "New York game" was played by two teams on a diamond-shaped field with bases ninety feet apart. One player in the middle of the diamond, forty-five feet from home base, served up pitches underhanded to opposing "strikers"; these batted in rotation and tried to pile up runs by hitting the ball and then circling the bases before defenders could ring up three outs, either by recording strikeouts or tagging runners or catching flies in the air or on one bounce. The first side to score twenty-one runs won the game. Cartwright's rules also established fair and foul areas and stipulated the duties of the single umpire. The Knickerbockers played nearly all their games among themselves until the early 1850s, since they strived to be sole proprietors of the new sport. But they did take on a group of picked opponents in a game at the Elysian Fields in Hoboken, on June 19, 1846.

Rival clubs soon imitated the Knickerbockers. Club members were expected to be men of means and social standing who paid dues, purchased uniforms, agreed to uphold standards of gentlemanly behavior, and resolved to pursue the sport as amateur hobbyists. Matches against other clubs were arranged by formal invitation and carried the air of a social occasion, perhaps as an English rowing regatta does today. By 1854 four clubs had formed in New York, the Knickerbockers, Gothams, Eagles, and Empires; and four others in Brooklyn, the Eckfords, Atlantics, Putnams, and Excelsiors.

In the second half of the decade other clubs continued to spring up in and around New York City, then throughout New York State and the rest of the East. By 1860 about 60 clubs had been created, among them the Philadelphia Athletics and teams as far west as Cleveland, St. Louis, Detroit, and Chicago. Some of the teams organized according to occupation, such as the New York Mutuals (firefighters) and Metropolitans (schoolteachers). Others were formed by colleges (e.g., Harvard in 1864, Yale in 1865; Williams and Amherst had played a "Massachusetts game" of baseball in 1859). In 1858 the National Association of Base Ball Players was created to establish guidelines for organizing all these new clubs and to disseminate newly agreed upon rules. The Association specified the size of balls and bats, standardized the nine-inning length of the game in 1858, created the pitcher's box in 1863, stipulated that batters could call for pitches in a certain area, and eliminated outs for flies caught on the bounce (except for fouls) in 1864. Though as a central authority the Association was rather feeble throughout the thirteen years of its existence, it did create some central authority for rules and therefore helped its particular version of the game to prevail. After the Civil War a mania developed around the sport: 91 clubs belonged to the Association in 1865, including fifteen members of a North Western Association that stretched from Kenyon College to Dubuque; 202 clubs from seventeen states were represented at the 1866 Association convention; and over 300 showed up in 1867, including members of nine clubs in Des Moines and several from towns in Minnesota. When twelve-year-old Albert G. Spalding moved to Rockford, Illinois (population 7000) in 1862, baseball was already established there.

As one would expect, the eastern teams dominated play on the field in the 1860s. The Brooklyn Excelsiors, led by star pitcher Jim Creighton, attracted a large following between 1859 and 1862, until Creighton (age 21) was fatally injured in the line of duty. The Excelsiors' tour of the East in 1860 established a pattern of such barnstorming and helped popularize the sport. The Brooklyn Eckfords won the mythical championship in 1862 and 1863. The Brooklyn Atlantics in one seven-year period won five championships, including undefeated seasons in 1864 and 1865, behind shortstop Dickie Pearce and first baseman Joe Start. Morrisania (with shortstop George Wright), Philadelphia's Athletics (behind second baseman Al Reach and pitcher Dick McBride), the New York Mutuals, and the Washington Nationals also fielded strong clubs. Western clubs were not long in catching up, however. When the Nationals toured the West in July 1867, they easily defeated teams in

Columbus, Cincinnati, Louisville, Indianapolis, and Chicago; but the Rockford Forest Cities, behind pitcher Spalding, upset them 28-23. By 1870 the Forest Cities themselves were barnstorming east and defeating nearly every opponent. Perhaps more important than questions of East-West dominance, however, was the quality of play. Fielders who positioned themselves cautiously on their respective bases now began to venture off their bags; runners began to slide to avoid tags; a pitcher named Arthur "Candy" Cummings developed a curveball in 1865; and barehanded fielders nevertheless became ever more surehanded.

The Rise of Professionalism

While the National Association tried to retain exclusive control of the game, two features of American life — competition and commercialization — were undermining gentlemanly ways. During the Civil War games between clubs were less frequent, but more and more Americans became acquainted with the game when soldiers played it. Forty thousand soldiers watched a Christmas Day game in 1862, and large crowds, sometimes exceeding 10,000 people, were not uncommon in the years just before and after the war. Newspapers began covering the games and even publishing rudimentary box scores. And more and more working-class men began playing.

With that increased popularity came professionalism. After all, strict amateurism can be sustained in a sport only when it is played as a diversion by a privileged minority. As interest in baseball increased, therefore, and with it the public's appreciation for expert play and winning teams, clubs began charging admission of willing patrons and using those admission charges to attract the best players, regardless of their social rank. Beginning as early as 1859, when the Excelsiors appear to have paid Jim Creighton, promoters were hunting up and recruiting talented players for their ability and paying for their services by sharing receipts (the best teams were able to charge 10 cents or 25 cents as early as 1863, and by 1868 the seven or eight most prominent teams were splitting as much as $100,000), by making direct salary payments (e.g., to Creighton and Al Reach), by offering jobs (e.g., Tammany Hall jobs supported the Mutuals, and most Washington Nationals held government jobs), or even by arranging "fixed" games (e.g., two Mutuals were expelled from the Association for fixing a September 1865 game). Players known as "revolvers" regularly moved from team to team, following the best offer. By 1869, the game had reached a sort of twilight state. Amateurs predominated, of course, since many hobbyists were still being attracted to the game. At the same time, however, many star players across the country were being paid. Indeed, at the 1869 Association convention Henry Chadwick admitted that baseball was a business, and teams on western barnstorming tours were regularly capitalizing on hometown boosterism and East-West rivalry (even as they spread interest in the game as well).

One of those touring clubs was organized in Cincinnati. Only this team was different: all ten players (only one a Cincinnatian) received salaries, ranging from $600 to $1400. Stung by embarrassing losses and anxious to foster civic pride, Cincinnati businessmen led by Aaron Champion enlisted the savvy Harry Wright, who had moved to Cincinnati after the Civil War as an instructor for the Union Cricket Club, to recruit a topnotch club to be known as the Red Stockings. During the 1869 season the Reds toured the nation from Atlantic to Pacific, attracting well over 100,000 spectators and dominating the opposition: their record was 57 wins, no losses, and one tie. Thanks to stars like Wright, his brother George, and pitcher Asa Brainard, the Reds also won their first 27 games in 1870 before being stopped on June 14 by the Brooklyn Atlantics, 8-7, in a sensational 11-inning game. Interest in the Reds diminished after that loss and another later in the year, so that investors only broke even; consequently, the club returned to amateurism for 1871 and the players scattered to teams in other cities.

Nevertheless, the Reds' success inspired imitators. By the end of 1870 at least five teams were completely salaried. Matters came to a head at the Association convention that preceded the 1871 season when amateurs staged a walkout; the professionals in March determined to begin a new association — the National Association of Professional Base Ball Players, the first professional league. The teams that entered — Philadelphia Athletics, Boston Red Stockings, Chicago White Stockings, Cleveland Forest Cities, Rockford Forest Cities, Troy Haymakers, Washington Olympics, New York Mutuals, and Ft. Wayne Kekiongas (who soon quit, replaced by the Brooklyn Eckfords) — agreed to play each other five times and to desist from raiding each other for player services. In the absence of a strong amateur association, the professionals gradually came to dominate organized baseball and to dictate rules and playing styles.

The pioneering National Association endured for five seasons. Philadelphia earned the first championship after a close and disputed race with runner-up Boston. The popular Chicago entry unfortunately was forced to finish its season on the road with borrowed equipment when on October 9 its 7000-seat park was destroyed in the Great Fire. It would be 1874 before the White Stockings could rejoin the Association. By 1872 Boston had begun to establish its domination over the league so thoroughly that fan interest fell and five discouraged rivals failed to play out their schedules. Having attracted the Wright brothers from Cincinnati, Harry as manager and George as star hitter, as well as infielder Ross Barnes and pitcher Al Spalding (both from Rockford), the Red Stockings won 39 and lost only 8. The race was closer in 1873 and only one entry dropped out, but Boston won again, and again in 1874 and 1875. Since games were played only two or three times a week, Spalding could pitch nearly every game, and manager Wright schooled the team in intelligent hitting and tight defense. On nearly every club now, specialists manned each position, teamwork improved so that double plays were common, and pitchers (though still required to throw underhand) had begun to perfect the curve and change of pace. Catchers, who previously had received pitches on the bound, began to move up closer to the batter with men on base. Offensively, aggressive hitting and baserunning reflected the professionals' commitment to winning instead of polite gentlemanly sport.

Boston's success on the field made the club a financial success, but the imbalance in competition made the league shakier and shakier. Furthermore, other flaws were becoming apparent in the administration of the player-operated circuit. Central control was so deficient that the league had no effective means of enforcing crowd control, resolving disputes, or disciplining drunken or dishonest players. Players still "revolved" freely from team to team, sometimes during the season. Playing rules were still not completely uniform. Gambling and rumors of fixed games undermined public confidence and patronage. The $10 league entrance fee made it easy for clubs to enter, but also made it easy for them to drop out, so league membership was loose and unpredictable. Financial arrangements for distributing gate receipts were inequitable and scheduling was haphazard, with each city scrambling to reserve for itself the most attractive playing dates and finding excuses not to visit weaker cities. The Boston Red Stockings and Philadelphia Athletics made a particular shambles of the 1874 schedule when Wright and Spalding led them on a tour of England in midseason in an effort to make money and spread Americanism. As a result of the tour, most teams were forced to pack games into the less profitable early and late seasons, and only one team completed its schedule.

After the example of Harry Wright, who capably handled all business affairs for Boston, professional managers were gradually being enlisted to take over administrative duties during these years; however, they failed to match Wright's success on or off the field. When Boston totally dominated play in 1875, with a 71-8 record, and when an economic downturn reduced attendance still further, the thirteen-member league touched bottom. Many clubs quit during the season (Keokuk after a 1-13 start; the Brooklyn Atlantics after going 2-42; and four others with a combined record of 17-88), and only Chicago and Philadelphia could compete with Boston at all.

The Birth of the National League

Boston's success nevertheless demonstrated what a stable, businesslike approach could accomplish; and Wright's tactics were not lost on William A. Hulbert, the ambitious new proprietor of the Chicago franchise. During the 1875 season, in preparation for 1876, Hulbert had signed the Athletics' Adrian "Cap" Anson, destined to become the top hitter of the nineteenth century, and several star Red Stockings: Spalding, Barnes, "Deacon" White, and Cal McVey. To protect his investment, Hulbert determined to stabilize the professional game. During the fall and winter of 1875-76, Hulbert hatched plans for a new league, secured the support of other western clubs in St. Louis, Louisville, and Cincinnati, and enlisted the tacit approval of Harry Wright. At a February 1876 meeting in New York, Hulbert laid out the blueprint for his new league before handpicked representatives from Boston, Hartford, New York, and Philadelphia, who readily agreed to its stipulations. The new National League of Professional Baseball Clubs (NL) placed administrative responsibilities with owners, not players, in an attempt to create a more stable arrangement. To enhance prospects for financial success, each franchise was given a limited monopoly: stringent entrance requirements kept marginal cities out; each city was granted exclusive rights to its own area; steps were taken to minimize revolving; and agreements were made on admission prices and disposition of gate receipts. At the same time, in moves reminiscent of its "gentlemanly" past, baseball magnates took steps to rehabilitate the image of the professional game in order to recapture public respect and patronage: umpires were to be paid; a central administration was established to keep records, handle disputes, and discipline players; and each club agreed to eliminate betting on its grounds and to refrain from playing on Sunday. The eight original clubs agreed to play ten games against each opponent, three games per week, during the 1876 season. The National League power play worked completely. Caught off guard, the National Association folded after brief opposition.

Nevertheless, the National League was not a quick success. Its first seasons were marked by financial struggle and instability. Bolstered by its new stars and managed by Spalding, Chicago easily topped runners-up St. Louis and Hartford and outscored its nearest rival by nearly 200 runs. But unequal competition (cellar-dwelling Cincinnati won just 9 of 65 games) discouraged fan support so much that the A's and New York Mutuals, anticipating poor gate receipts, did not make their final trip west. This challenge to the new league's authority was beaten back when both teams were expelled, but the league now had to make do with six teams and no representatives in the two largest eastern cities. In 1877 Boston regained the crown as Chicago fell to fifth. Manager Spalding, now 27, quit pitching and moved to first base, and the next season began to devote even more energy to his fledgling sporting goods empire. He was already supplying the league with balls and publishing Spalding's Official Baseball Guide, with Chadwick soon serving as editor and lending his support to the new league. Louisville provided strong competition until star pitcher Jim Devlin and three others conspired to fix games and give Boston the championship. All four were barred from the league, and the Louisville team then disbanded. St. Louis and Hartford — which had played all but one of its home games in Brooklyn anyway — also dropped out, and the league took in Providence, Indianapolis, and Milwaukee for 1878 (these last two surviving just the one season).

In 1878 Boston won Harry Wright's last pennant, beating surprising Cincinnati, but the league continued to struggle at the gate. Distrusted after the Louisville scandal, lacking franchises in major cities like New York and Philadelphia, and hurting from a national economic depression that reached its nadir in 1878, the league staggered into the 1879 season with four more new franchises in Troy, Syracuse, Cleveland, and Buffalo joining four holdovers. Providence, behind George Wright's leadership, John Montgomery Ward's pitching, and "Orator" Jim O'Rourke's hitting, won the championship by five games over Boston, but the season was another financial flop. Syracuse, Troy, Cleveland, and Buffalo all left the league within five seasons, and Boston fired Harry Wright in the hopes of somehow turning its financial fortunes. Moreover, struggling ownership placed financial restrictions on players to try to reduce losses. Salaries were lowered, players were charged for uniforms, and a reserve system was instituted to prevent players from earning higher wages elsewhere.

Complicating the National League's development was competition with other baseball clubs. It should be remembered that there were significant other leagues and teams in the 1870s apart from the National Association and National League, all of which considered themselves rivals, not minor leagues. While professional leagues struggled to survive, college teams sprang up everywhere, and independent pro and semipro clubs regularly played each other as well as league teams in exhibitions. The best of these teams competed on an equal footing with teams from the National Association and National League both on the field and at the box office. For example, well established independent teams in Cincinnati and Louisville were ready to join when Hulbert formed his league in 1876. The Indianapolis Hoosiers of 1877 were the best team in the League Alliance when they were invited to join the National League. A team from Worcester was good enough to join the league intact in 1880 after Syracuse folded, and the New York Metropolitans played 151 games in 1881, many against National League teams. The New York Mutuals, Philadelphia A's, and St. Louis Reds all remained in existence after leaving the National League in the 1870s. National League clubs raided such teams for players, but they also competed against them for public support. By the close of 1879, the future of the National League seemed most uncertain.

The Professional Game Comes of Age

At this juncture, however, National League fortunes began to improve substantially. Its sober efforts to achieve respectability, the attractiveness of talented stars, more balanced competition, stable leadership, and (not least important) a sharply improving national economy all combined to introduce the prosperity of which Hulbert had dreamed.

On the field the Chicago White Stockings dominated the first half of the decade. When Spalding moved to the front office, Anson took over managerial duties in 1879, and under his direction and with the support of his powerful bat, the Sox won five pennants by 1886. A strapping 200-pounder born in a log cabin in Iowa, Anson never finished worse than sixth in the league in batting from 1876 through 1889 and finished his 22-year NL career with over 3000 hits, an amazing total considering the far shorter schedules conventional in the nineteenth century and his uncredited five-year stint in the National Association. Moreover, he helped to assemble a formidable supporting cast that included pitcher John Clarkson, who registered 160 wins between 1885 and 1888, and flamboyant outfielder Mike "King" Kelly, a clever hitter and daring baserunner with a fondness for liquor, horses, and scoring runs.

The popular White Stockings won by fifteen games in 1880 as Providence fell to second. In 1881 Chicago again prevailed, this time by nine games over Providence and ten over Buffalo. Before the 1882 season Hulbert died and Spalding took over as Chicago's chief executive (where he remained until 1905), but the team was unaffected, winning by three games over Providence and ten over Boston. Boston captured the 1883 flag, though, by four games over the White Stockings, and Providence won a championship in 1884, thanks largely to the heroism of Charles "Old Hoss" Radbourne. Pressed into almost daily service when the team's other pitcher quit after being disciplined for drinking on the job, Radbourne pitched an astounding 678 innings and won 60 of 72 decisions, 18 of them in a row.

Chicago reclaimed the crown in 1885 and 1886, turning back determined opposition and attracting large crowds. The 1885 flag was a product mostly of Clarkson's 53 wins and a great September pennant drive that overtook New York's two pitching stars, Mickey Welch (44-11) and Tim Keefe (32-13). Anson's 147 RBIs (in 125 games) lifted his aging team to one last championship in 1886 over runner-up Detroit, whose own slugger Dan Brouthers hit .370 with 11 homers. King Kelly batted .388, but his drinking led to a confrontation with Anson, after which he was sold to Boston for the astounding price of $10,000. Detroit prevailed in 1887, having purchased Brouthers and other Buffalo stars when that team folded in 1885. And New York won in 1888 and 1889 behind Monte Ward, now a shortstop, first baseman Roger Connor, catcher William "Buck" Ewing, and its overpowering pitching. Over 200,000 fans came to watch the 1889 Giants, who turned a staggering profit.

The White Stockings and Giants were not the only teams that prospered in the 1880s. Boston reportedly cleared $13,000 in 1885 against receipts of $40,000 or so, and an incredible $48,000 in 1883. Though the franchise ran into trouble later in the decade, Detroit earned $12,000 in 1881 out of gross receipts of $35,000. In several cities new wooden parks were constructed, and by the mid-'80s crowds of 10,000 were not uncommon.

Rival Major Leagues

Not surprisingly, this new prosperity encouraged rivals and interlopers, especially among clubs barred from the National League. When Cincinnati was expelled from the league in 1880 for insisting on offering beer in the stands and Sunday ball to a German population accustomed to a continental Sabbath, its owners actively plotted a new league. With other rivals ever ready in the wings, the new American Association (AA) quickly took shape, placing teams in Cincinnati, Louisville, St. Louis, Baltimore, Pittsburgh, and Philadelphia for the 1882 season. The new association copied the older league except in a few respects: it permitted Sunday games and exhibitions during the season; it insisted on a 25¢ admission charge as against the NL's 50¢; and, always more colorful and freewheeling then its stodgy and respectable elder and featuring several brewmasters as owners, it permitted beer and whiskey to be sold in the stands. One such owner, in fact, a colorful, erratic, and ultimately tragic St. Louis beer garden impresario named Chris Von der Ahe, viewed baseball as only one of several schemes for increasing his liquor sales.

With franchises in large cities and well-heeled investors, the American Association immediately competed for the best players and offered top-notch competition, Cincinnati capturing its first flag behind star second baseman Bid McPhee. In response to this solid threat, the National League restored franchises to New York and Philadelphia after the 1882 season, lopping off its smallest and weakest markets, Troy and Worcester. (The NL further strengthened itself in 1885 by replacing Buffalo and Providence with Washington and Kansas City.) After a profitable 1883 season, the Philadelphia Athletics winning the AA pennant, the two leagues patched together an uneasy and temporary peace. Each agreed to quit raiding the other for players and to observe the restrictions of the reserve rule. The league champions also agreed informally to a postseason exhibition series, a series that became an institution through 1891.

The American Association profited for a time under this arrangement. It fielded twelve teams for 1884 (in part to coopt the intrusions of the newly formed Union Association) — its original six plus the New York Mets (the eventual league champion), Columbus, Indianapolis, Washington, Brooklyn, and Toledo — and then dropped back to a more manageable and competitive eight in 1885. By that time St. Louis under Von der Ahe and manager Charles Comiskey had put together the makings of a dynasty. With third baseman Arlie Latham leading a tight defense and outfielder Tip O'Neill commanding the offense, the Browns won four straight championships. Furthermore, St. Louis bested the White Stockings in the series played after the 1885 and 1886 seasons, at the height of the AA, and barely lost to the National League champions in 1887 and 1888. In 1889 the Brooklyn Bridegrooms narrowly (and controversially, since one of their victories was a forfeit by St. Louis, under protest) topped the Browns. Louisville prevailed in 1890, and Boston won the last AA flag in 1891.

A number of factors combined to kill the American Association. Despite the "peace" between the leagues, competition for players remained keen throughout the decade, and player salaries therefore escalated sharply. As a result weaker franchises were hard pressed to keep up on the field and in their financial ledgers, especially under the pressure of the low 25¢ admission price. The more stable and prestigious National League began to attract defectors, Pittsburgh after 1885 and others later. Gradually the American Association became polarized between the very strong franchises in St. Louis and Brooklyn and weaker ones nearly everywhere else. By 1889 Louisville could win only 27 of 138 games, other teams were not much better, and the best players had gradually gravitated to the National League. Terrible spring weather in 1889 flooded fields and discouraged fans still further. The National League began to press its advantage, particularly after the newly formed Players League folded in 1890. Because of its richer franchises the older league won nearly every skirmish for players, Pittsburgh earning a team nickname by "pirating" Louis Bierbauer. The crisis facing the Association created infighting, and when a new league president was selected by one faction, Cincinnati and Brooklyn in 1890 bolted to the National League, thereby reducing the AA, in effect, to a minor league. (The terrible 1889 Louisville team rose to the 1890 pennant merely because it was able to retain its players in the face of other AA teams' defections.) After the 1891 season Baltimore, St. Louis, Washington, and Louisville were absorbed into an expanded, twelve-team National League, the other franchises were bought out, and the AA folded its tent and vanished.

The American Association was not the only rival of the National League. Ever since the demise of the player-led National Association, many players had longed to restore their lost hegemony, especially during a period when captains of industry and baseball club owners alike tended to look upon employees as chattels and did all they could to reduce salaries. When the reserve rule, which essentially enabled teams, if they chose, to "reserve" a contracted player's services forever, was drafted in the depressed year 1879, it was rationalized as a measure necessary to preserve competitive balance and a sane salary structure. When the system was continued and expanded to cover not just five players but as many as eleven (by 1883), the players looked upon it as a means to keep the price of labor down when skilled players were in demand. The Union Association, so called because it disdained the reserve clause, offered players one alternative for 1884, but when St. Louis bought up the best players and won 94 of its 113 games, the league folded for lack of fan interest. Still, the rivalry between the National League and American Association tended to inflate salaries more than the owners liked, so the two leagues agreed to hold salaries to a $2000 maximum for 1886 and to charge players for uniforms and 50¢ per day for road trip expenses.

While that agreement was often ignored, it still infuriated the players, who turned for redress to their own National Brotherhood of Professional Baseball Players. Founded in October 1885 as a benevolent organization dedicated to caring for sick and needy players, the Brotherhood had by 1887 attracted 90 members who were now committed to bargaining in their own interests. The abuse of the reserve rule and the salary cap were only two issues important to the Brotherhood, which was led by John Montgomery Ward, a respected star player and shrewdly politic Columbia University Law School graduate. As Ward explained in an essay entitled "Is the Base Ball Player a Chattel?", the players also objected to being sold or traded without their permission and without profiting themselves from the sale, as had once been customary. Like other workers of the period, they wished to have a voice in disciplinary disputes, to be paid while recuperating from injury or illness, and to eliminate the notorious practice of blacklisting, a favorite tactic of nineteenth-century industrialists. Clubs regularly blacklisted players for off-the-field indiscretions, for insubordination, or for signing with rival teams (including those in the Union Association). At first the Brotherhood was greeted civilly by owners, who agreed to eliminate maximum salaries for 1888; the players in turn promised better behavior. But while Ward was away on a world exhibition baseball tour led by Spalding during the winter of 1888-89, the owners reinstated a maximum salary and even proposed to pay players according to skill grades from A to E. When counternegotiations during the 1889 season failed, the players determined to form their own league.

The Players League (PL) was formally ratified on November 5, 1889.

An alliance between workers and owners, both of whom shared governance and agreed to distribute equally each team's profit after investors claimed the first $10,000, the league quickly established franchises and secured playing sites in all National League cities except Cincinnati. Just as important, the PL signed up nearly every star player, including Ward, Kelly, Ewing, Comiskey, Connor, Keefe, Radbourne, and Brouthers, and won several court battles against the reserve rule. Players League backers even arranged to purchase the Cincinnati franchise after the 1890 season.

Prospects for the new league therefore appeared very favorable, but the National League counterattacked vigorously. The NL induced some players to jump back, waged an aggressive campaign in the press, scheduled many of its games opposite the PL's, and wooed fans with free tickets and other promotions. With ticket prices slashed through ruinous competition, attendance soared in both leagues. The Players League, with Boston winning the flag, probably outdrew its rival by about 10 percent, but neither adversary could profit. On the verge of success but confronted by financial losses, several PL owners panicked and sued for peace to the NL, which divided its rival owners and therefore conquered. Their ranks broken, the players could do little but try to negotiate a settlement; however, the "compromise" worked out left the reserve system intact and a salary cap in place. Even worse, by attracting players and fans the PL mortally wounded the already struggling American Association, which folded after one more season and thereby dealt the players another blow. By the end of 1891 the National League had regained its monopoly over major league professional ball.

The Game in the 1880s

All this competition among leagues did not seem to hinder developments around and within the game itself. On the contrary, by 1890 most rituals and tactics associated with modern baseball were solidly entrenched. Although the ever-respectable National League's fairly steep 50¢ admission charge and afternoon starting times ensured that most spectators would be relatively well-to-do professional males, a cross section of society was nevertheless represented in the stands. This was especially evident when Ladies Days became common in the 1880s (in part to amend unruly crowd behavior), when the American Association admitted fans for a quarter and catered to the working class with

Sunday games, and when National League clubs began opening their bleachers or offering standing room in the outfield at reduced prices. After passing through the turnstiles, fans sat in wooden, semi-permanent grandstands — until a series of fires around the turn of the century encouraged the construction of permanent steel and concrete structures. Once in their seats, patrons could count on being comfortable. Frankfurters, other foods, soft drinks, and beer and whiskey (in AA cities) were on sale. Musicians often entertained before games, between innings, and between games of doubleheaders. Invented by Chadwick in the 1860s, scorecards were available for those so inclined. And players by 1890 had ceased selling tickets and working the gate, and had begun practicing hitting and fielding before the game — activities that were becoming flashy attractions in themselves.

Once the games began, fans of the 1880s could count on seeing contests very similar to the ones later played by Mathewson, Medwick, and Mays. Basic rules affecting the number of players per side and the means for scoring runs and recording outs had been codified before professional teams formed. The basic uniform — knickers, stockings, shirt, cap — had become conventional by the early 1870s. Basic tactics like catcher's and coach's signs, pitchouts and brush backs, relays and cutoffs, were widely practice before 1890. Popups, passed balls, fungoes, grounders, assists, balks, walks, and whitewashes were all part of the game's lexicon. Hillerich began manufacturing customized bats in Louisville by 1884, and batters waited to hit in on-deck circles. The size, weight, and composition of the ball had been made relatively consistent with modern standards by Spalding's company, although "dead" and "live" versions of the ball were in circulation. Infielders stationed themselves as modern players do, shortstops and second basemen flanking second base, and first- and third-basemen away from their bags, after the "fair-foul hit" was outlawed in 1877. (Before that time any hit that touched fair ground even once was ruled fair no matter where it then went, so fielders on the corners had to stick close to their bases where they could cover "foul" ground.) Bench jockeying was considered standard behavior, and everyone berated the umpires, one of whom typically supervised a game alone until the early 1880s. A couple of minor league teams even experimented with night baseball, but the new electric lights were not yet up to the task.

Of course the game was also different in certain respects. Most fielders disdained the use of gloves until the 1880s, when they wore modest kid gloves. Catchers wisely stayed far behind the batter unless a runner was aboard because (a) it was safer there and (b) a foul ball caught on one bounce was an out before 1879. When that rule was discarded and the mask, chest protector, and overstuffed glove were developed (all by the late 1880s), catchers began to squat closer and closer to the batter. The pitcher's box remained just 45 feet from home until 1881, when the distance was lengthened by five feet, and pitchers were given from five to nine balls (depending on the specific season) before a walk was awarded. But they were also required to pitch underhand, and until 1887 a batter could request high or low pitches. Sidearm pitching began to encroach on professional play in the early 1870s and overhand pitching was permitted in the more innovative American Association in 1883 (National Leaguers were permitted to throw overhand in 1884). Clubs scheduled games two or three times a week: the National League played under 100 games a season until 1884, when competition among leagues forced them to seek additional revenues through expanding their schedules and cutting back on exhibitions with independent clubs. By 1888 the major leagues scheduled 140 games. Since one or two pitchers could cover the shorter schedules and since no substitutions were permitted once a game began, except in the case of injuries and illnesses certified by the opposition, rosters consisted of only a dozen or so players through the 1880s.

Between seasons and after games, fans could still follow their favorite teams closely. Afte 1876 baseball guides appeared each winter with summaries and statistics. *The Sporting News* began publishing in 1886 and by 1889 had enlisted over 60,000 subscribers. Each summer day newspapers carried box scores and game stories to satisfy the appetites of fans, for already the fortunes of the local team were a source of civic pride or embarrassment and a lively source of conversation. Because of local partisanship and the game's gentlemanly traditions, sportswriters lent a moral tone to their reporting, with hometown heroes created and described in lofty jargon. Lionized players were rewarded with gifts, celebrations, and adulation. Popular players endorsed products, especially sporting goods, and were featured on picture cards as early as 1868. Several teams (though not all) trained in the South during the springs of the 1880s, as much to strike public relations fires as to condition bodies.

Most professional players nevertheless led lives as insecure as other workers of the era. Many battled insolvency, illiteracy, and drunkenness as fiercely as opposing teams. Hulbert died in 1882 shortly after banning ten players for chronic drinking. Injury or illness or a capricious owner could also end a career at any time, yet the playing season was so long that obtaining offseason employment or preparing for a post-retirement career was difficult. Stories were legion of former players who became dissolute or destitute, or who died early.

Most players hailed from the East or Midwest, where baseball was especially popular; of the 168 major league players active in 1887, 34 came from Pennsylvania, 31 from Massachusetts, 20 from Ohio, 19 from New York, and most of the rest from adjoining areas. Southern European immigrants did not warm to the sport as readily as the Irish and Germans, who took up the game in large numbers as the century wore on, or as much as the white, Anglo-Saxon Protestants who dominated player ranks during the "gentlemanly" days before 1876. Still, the game was a national sport by the 1880s, and by proving themselves on college, sandlot, or minor league teams (a rudimentary farm system was already being formed by some big league teams), a player from any region or nationality could reach the major leagues.

Unless the player was black, that is. By 1890 a color barrier was firmly in place that would keep black players out of white professional leagues for nearly sixty years. Originally, only four years after the Emancipation Proclamation, the gentlemanly National Association of Base Ball Players banned "persons of color" from their clubs. However, democratic forces that asserted themselves during reconstruction soon enabled more than 60 black players to join professional teams, mostly in the West, mostly in fringe leagues, and mostly in a sporadic and often second-class fashion. Moses Fleetwood "Fleet" Walker, who had played college baseball at Oberlin and the University of Michigan, caught for Toledo of the Northwest League in 1883. When Toledo joined the American Association in 1884, Walker became the first black major leaguer. The Toledo franchise collapsed in 1885, but Walker was joined by several other black players (including Frank Grant, probably the best nineteenth-century black player) in the International League, the Ohio State League, and other circuits for the rest of the decade. Integrated baseball was nipped in the bud, however, when white teammates objected, when opponents tried to intimidate blacks, and when star white players (most notoriously, Cap Anson in 1887) refused to take the field against blacks in exhibitions. A few black players persisted after 1890, and John McGraw even attempted to employ Charles Grant on his 1901 Baltimore team by passing him off as an Indian, but integrated professional teams were extinct by 1898. Instead, and in keeping with

Jim Crow customs, black players organized their own teams. The earliest black clubs had been organized in the 1860s, and by the late 1880s all-black teams were playing throughout the country, including the South, and the first salaried black teams had been organized after the example of the independent Cuban Giants, who began play in 1885. By 1887 a seven-team professional black league had been formed; though it survived barely a week, contemporary black clubs often defeated college, semi-pro, professional, and even major league teams in exhibitions.

The 1890s

Ironically, the demise of the Players League and the American Association did not bring prosperity to the National League. Yet another American monopoly in the age of national trusts, the NL nonetheless struggled to scratch out a profit, and its players suffered depressed salaries. Competition on the field continued to advance, however, because the consolidation of teams at the end of the PL and AA eliminated marginal players and because a new generation of star players was ready to assert itself.

Traditional powerhouses in St. Louis and Chicago lost their prominence on the field during the 1890s, and all of the pennants were won by Frank Selee's Boston Beaneaters or Ned Hanlon's Baltimore and Brooklyn teams. Selee attracted so many stars to Boston when the PL and AA folded that the club won five pennants in the decade and competed strongly in the other seasons. King Kelly, who piloted the Boston PL entry and then moved briefly to the AA, ended up with the Beaneaters at the end of 1891 and, with Bobby Lowe and Charles "Kid" Nichols, helped push them to the championship. Nichols that year began a string of seven consecutive 30-win seasons. Hugh Duffy arrived in 1892 and scored 125 runs. In the meantime, with the league now swollen to twelve teams as a result of the AA settlement, an experimental split-season format was devised to keep fans interested all summer and to provide a grounds for continuing the tradition of post-season playoff series. Boston so easily won the first half that, when Cleveland won the second, the Beaneaters were accused of relaxing. The charge seemed well grounded, for Boston easily swept the playoffs after a memorable 11-inning opener, when Nichols and Denton "Cyclone" Young pitched a scoreless tie. Since attendance fell by some 300,000 in the second half, the split-season idea was scrapped for 1893.

Boston again won by a comfortable margin, Duffy scoring 147 times, even though Philadelphia's sensational Ed Delahanty (one of the finest righthanded hitters of all time) slugged 19 homers and drove in 146 runs.

Baltimore's domination began in 1894 when manager and part owner Hanlon put together perhaps the finest team of the century. A perennial doormat in the American Association, Baltimore was one of the four clubs absorbed into the NL after 1891. Overcoming mediocre pitching, the team now distinguished itself through great offense, skillful defense, and intelligent play on the part of several future Hall of Famers and six future managers. Amos Rusie nearly pitched New York to the 1894 flag with a 2.78 ERA that was almost a full run better than his nearest competitor, but Baltimore nipped the Giants by one game because every Oriole regular batted over .300 and drove in at least 92 runs. Aging Dan Brouthers hit nine home runs and drove in 128 runs; catcher Wilbert Robinson batted .353; and left fielder Joe Kelley hit .393. After a slow start in 1895 Baltimore roared past Cleveland, with fiery third baseman John McGraw hitting .369 and stealing 61 bases, and Hugh Jennings batting .386, knocking in 125 runs, and leading all shortstops in chances, double plays, and fielding percentage. Nor could Cleveland's Cy Young or Jesse Burkett (who hit over .410 for the second straight year) derail Baltimore in 1896, since Jennings hit .401, Kelley .364, and 5'4" right fielder "Wee Willie" Keeler .392. The Orioles scored nearly 1000 runs in 129 games by combining power, speed, savvy, and the roughhouse style embodied by McGraw. Quintessential professionals, driven to win, and scornful of any vestiges of baseball's gentlemanly traditions, the Orioles epitomized social darwinism and survival of the fittest. Behind the quiet, intelligent Keeler they perfected place hitting, bunting, and the squeeze play. They practiced the double steal and hit and run play, and even engineered their home grounds to their own advantage. They reputedly filed their spikes before games and blocked runners from bases. So dominant and domineering were the Orioles in both substance and style that when power-hitting Boston edged Baltimore in 1897, despite Keeler's .432 average, and again in 1898, many fans tried to interpret events as the triumph of traditional values over coldly efficient professionalism.

Baltimore, however, prevailed over Boston in the final Temple Cup series after the 1897 season. The series, named for a Pittsburgh sportsman who sponsored the series and offered a prize, is sometimes considered as a precursor of the modern World Series, but it failed after four years of matching first- and second-place teams. The series never really captured the public imagination because unmotivated champions usually played listlessly against runners-up, who won three of the four series.

While Boston and Baltimore thrived in the won-loss columns, the whole league suffered financially. The costly wars with the AA and PL left the league in debt. With twelve teams now in the circuit, competition was inevitably unequal. Washington, St. Louis, and Louisville had just one winning season among them during the entire decade, and St. Louis won just 29 of 131 games in 1897. League members in essence fell into two groups: one comprised of four or five relatively healthy franchises that attracted most of the fans, and another made up of the struggling have-nots. In 1897 New York attracted about 2500 fans to each game, but Cleveland averaged only about 460, even with popular Penobscot Indian Louis Sockalexis in the outfield. By 1899 Cleveland was winning only 20 of 154 games, drawing under 200 fans per contest, and choosing to finish the season exclusively on the road. Financial matters were not helped by a general economic depression that struck the nation in 1893 and continued through most of the decade.

Faced with such difficulties, the league experimented with a number of remedies. The split season came and went in 1892, and the longer, 154-game schedule was adopted for the 1898 season. Most teams were permitted to play Sunday ball, at least on the road, so that by 1899 only Boston refused to play on the Sabbath.

Owners also resolved to create a more exciting game offensively. With the twenty-four major-league teams playing in 1890 reduced to a dozen, weaker pitchers were weeded out and those that remained began dominating hitters. On Boston's 1891 champions, no one batted higher than .288. Hugh Duffy's .301 mark led the Beaneaters in 1892, and King Kelly could manage only an embarrasing .189. Thus for the 1893 season the pitcher's rubber replaced the pitcher's box and was positioned 60'6" from home plate — and runs per game increased over 25 percent. Strikeouts dropped in half. The number of .300 hitters, having fallen to nine in 1891, rose to fifty-one in 1894. Duffy won the triple crown in 1894 with a .438 average, 18 homers, and 145 RBI. And Boston now was scoring so many runs that its 1894 season total has never been topped. Earned run averages soared, and some pitchers never got over the change: for example, the White Stockings' Bill Hutchinson, who won 122 games between 1890 and 1892, fell to 16 in 1893. Pitchers gradually adjusted, however, and developed more subtle deliveries — better curves and screwballs, more deceptive changes of pace. The increased pitching distance and longer schedules also forced teams to add more pitchers, so that by the end of the century teams carried from five to eight well-rested hurlers. After the previous decade's experimentation, the four-ball, three-strike convention was the standard during the decade. The designation of a lone substitute was allowed for strategic purposes in 1891, and free substitution followed the year after. At the turn of the century the league began to count foul balls as strikes and adopted the pentagon-shaped home plate as an aid to umpires.

League members also responded to their financial trials by forcing players to accept more and more trying conditions. Some players were deprived of their jobs when rosters were pared to a maximum of thirteen in 1892, though numbers later increased. More important, long-term contracts were eliminated, and in 1894 a $2400 salary ceiling was adopted. With the reinstitution of the reserve clause and without recourse to rival leagues, players had little bargaining power. Amos Rusie, having singlehandedly hurled his Giants into contention in 1894 and having led the league in strikeouts and shutouts in 1895, sat out the 1896 season rather than accept a salary cut. As his team sank in the standings, Rusie took his case to court, but ownership remained firm and he had no choice but to accept terms for 1897. Cap Anson, in the twilight of his career but still a .300 hitter, finally quit baseball after the 1897 season, complaining that "baseball as at present conducted is a gigantic monopoly intolerant of opposition and run on a grab-all-there-is-in-sight basis that is alienating its friends and disgusting the very public that has so long and cheerfully supported it."

Part of what Anson objected to was "syndicatism," a scheme for creating pocket trusts within the baseball trust that grew up after 1885. Andrew Freedman, a headstrong, crafty, and aggressive millionaire with links to Tammany Hall, bought the Giants in 1895 and in the absence of strong central leadership created turmoil in the league for the rest of the decade. Among other things, Freedman attempted to reinforce and formalize a developing system of interlocking ownerships. Several other NL owners already held pieces of the Giants and engineered the franchise in suspicious ways to make sure a strong team was representing New York. Moreover, so many other owners held interests in so many other franchises that competition was becoming a farce. After the 1898 season, Baltimore owners Harry Vonderhorst, Charles Ebbets, and Ned Hanlon — who also owned controlling interests in Brooklyn — decided to shift Hanlon and most of his stars to Brooklyn where a larger population and a new ballpark promised greater potential for profits. Similar plans were being hatched further west. St. Louis owner Frank Robison, who also owned the Cleveland club, transferred the best Cleveland players to St. Louis. The moves decimated the Spiders, whose fans boycotted the team, and ended the dynasty of the Orioles, even though new manager John McGraw for a time kept the team competitive by batting .391 and finding a rookie pitching star, Joe McGinnity. St. Louis finished a disappointing fifth, even though former Spiders Burkett and Young batted .402 and won 26 games, respectively. But the revamped Brooklyn Superbas, already known locally as the Trolley Dodgers, rode former Orioles Kelley, Keeler, and Jennings to the 1899 pennant.

After the 1899 season the syndicators decided to consolidate their interests further. This time they jettisoned Cleveland and Baltimore completely, shifting McGinnity to Brooklyn and McGraw to St. Louis, and lopped off perennial weak sisters Washington and Louisville as well. Louisville owner Barney Dreyfuss was permitted to purchase Pittsburgh, and he brought with him star outfielder Fred Clarke and promising youngster Honus Wagner. The new eight-team league held a successful 1900 season, nearly every club showing healthy profits. On the field the Superbas won another pennant over resurgent Pittsburgh, as Wagner (a right fielder) batted .381 and led the league in doubles and triples. Clarke and especially Wagner also starred in the following seasons as Pittsburgh won three consecutive pennants — in 1902 by an incredible 28-game margin.

The NL decision in 1901 to shut down in four cities opened the way, however, for Ban Johnson, the capable if autocratic Western Association president, to act on his ambition to create a second major league. A native Cincinnatian and former reporter, Johnson systematically strengthened the Western Association after taking over in 1894. He convinced Cincinnati manager Charles Comiskey to take over the St. Paul entry and consolidated his strength elsewhere. When the National League reduced itself to eight cities, Johnson was ready. In October 1899 he renamed his circuit the American League, placed a franchise in vacated Cleveland, and helped Comiskey move his club to Chicago. With teams also in Detroit, Kansas City, Minneapolis, Indianapolis, and Milwaukee, the American League drew well during the 1900 season.

Late in 1900 Johnson declared open war on the National League. Announcing that his league would be "major," he first dropped Minneapolis, Kansas City, and Indianapolis and placed teams for the first time in eastern markets — in Boston, Baltimore, Washington, and Philadelphia (under Connie Mack). Next, he raided the National League for players, who welcomed the chance for salaries higher than the $2400 NL ceiling. Comiskey took several Chicago NL players across town and won the first AL pennant behind pitcher-manager Clark Griffith. Cy Young and Jimmy Collins jumped to the second place Boston Pilgrims; Joe McGinnity, John McGraw, and Wilbert Robinson returned to Baltimore; and Philadelphia's Nap Lajoie won the new league's triple crown playing for Mack. Skirmishes between the two leagues continued throughout 1901 and 1902. When the Phillies went to court to retain Lajoie he was simply transferred to Cleveland and avoided arrest by staying out of Pennsylvania. The Orioles, themselves raided by the NL, soon moved to New York and into direct competition with the Giants and their new manager John McGraw; nicknamed the Highlanders, they later became known as the Yankees. Milwaukee in the meantime moved to St. Louis. And competition for players continued. The new league survived challenges throughout the 1902 season, as Mack's Athletics topped St. Louis and Boston behind the pitching of George "Rube" Waddell and Eddie Plank.

By the end of the 1902 season the American League had secured a host of substantial players and the National League was seeking peace. Johnson would accept no treaty that failed to acknowledge his league as major or to permit it to keep virtually all disputed players, and the NL finally capitulated on the condition that the struggling Detroit franchise would not be moved to Pittsburgh to compete with the Pirates. The new National Agreement hammered out in Cincinnati in January 9-12, 1903 established separate but equal major leagues under the supervision of a three-man National Commission. The two leagues agreed to respect each other's contracts, to adopt the same playing rules, and to cooperate in the scheduling of games. Steps were also taken to protect minor league franchises, including the adoption of a draft system for players and the establishment of teams' right to reserve players. And the two leagues also agreed to match their champions after each season in a World Championship Series.

The triumph of the upstart American League turned out to be a blessing in disguise for the National League and for baseball in general. The rivalry between leagues stimulated public interest, and competition within two eight-team leagues proved more equitable than it had under the twelve-team National League. The agreement between the leagues signaled the end of professional baseball's experimental infancy. With stability in league administration and business affairs, with the arrival of a set of stable rules and conventions, and with league franchises firmly placed in cities they would occupy for the next half century, the game had reached maturity in the auspicious first years of a new century.

For More Information

The standard histories of nineteenth-century baseball, to which this summary is also much indebted, are David Q. Voigt's *American Baseball: From Gentleman's Sport to the Commissioner System* (1966; rpt. University Park, Pennsylvania, 1983), Harold Seymour's *Baseball: The Early Years* (New York, 1966), and Preston Orem's *Baseball: 1845-1881* (Altadena, CA, 1961). Informative though often fanciful is A. G. Spalding's *America's National Game* (New York, 1911). The finest collection of photographs on baseball before 1900 is very likely the 1984 issue of SABR's *The National Pastime*, edited by John Thorn and Mark Rucker. Details on particular years are available through microfilmed issues of *The Sporting News* (after 1886) and *Sporting Life*. Anton Grobani's bibliography, *A Guide to Baseball Literature* (Detroit, 1975) catalogues many primary and secondary sources. The New York Public Library contains the A. G. Spalding collection of thousands of books, pamphlets, periodicals, scrapbooks, records, letters, and photographs related to nineteenth-century baseball, as well as the papers of Harry Wright and Henry Chadwick. The Library of the National Baseball Hall of Fame in Cooperstown, New York, also has a large collection of primary materials.

For their helpful advice on earlier versions of this manuscript, hearty thanks to Ronald Smith, A. G. Stephenson, and especially John Thorn.